Tide Pools

Laura Marsh

NATIONAL
GEOGRAPHIC

Washington, D.C.

For Susan F. Zaleski —L.F.M.

Designed by Yay! Design

Library of Congress Cataloging-in-Publication Data

Names: Marsh, Laura F., author. | National Geographic Kids (Firm), publisher. | National Geographic Society (U.S.)
Title: Tide pools / by Laura Marsh.
Description: Washington, DC : National Geographic Kids, [2019] | Series: National geographic readers | Audience: Age 4-6. | Audience: Grade pre-school, excluding K.
Identifiers: LCCN 2018036068 (print) | LCCN 2018038678 (ebook) | ISBN 9781426333453 (e-book) | ISBN 9781426333460 (e-book + audio) | ISBN 9781426333439 (paperback) | ISBN 9781426333446 (hardcover)
Subjects: LCSH: Tide pool ecology--Juvenile literature. | Tide pool animals--Juvenile literature.
Classification: LCC QH541.5.S35 (ebook) | LCC QH541.5.S35 M37 2019 (print) | DDC 577.69/9--dc23
LC record available at https://lccn.loc.gov/2018036068

The author and publisher gratefully acknowledge the expert content review of this book by Susan F. Zaleski, Biological Oceanographer, Pacific Region, Bureau of Ocean Energy Management, and the literacy review of this book by Mariam Jean Dreher, professor of reading education, University of Maryland, College Park.

Author's note:
The title page shows a bat star and many red sea urchins in a tide pool in British Columbia, Canada. The table of contents page features a striped shore crab in Malibu, California.

Photo Credits
Cover, Craig Tuttle/Getty Images; 1, Peter Essick/Getty Images; 3, MYN/Sheri Mandel/Nature Picture Library; 4, Charlie Blacker/Shutterstock; 6-9, Andia/UIG via Getty Images; 10-11, Ryan Newton/Getty Images; 12 (UP), Serge Vero/Alamy Stock Photo; 12 (CTR LE), MYN/JP Lawrence/Nature Picture Library; 12 (CTR RT), Stuart Wilson/Science Source; 12 (LO), Troscha/Shutterstock; 13, Georgette Douwma/Getty Images; 14, Kelpfish/Dreamstime; 15 (UP), George Grall/National Geographic Creative; 15 (LO LE), James Forte/National Geographic Creative; 15 (LO RT), DeeAnn Cranston/Shutterstock; 16, George Grall/National Geographic Creative; 17 (UP), Tim Laman/National Geographic Creative; 17 (LO), Michael Hoyer/Alamy Stock Photo; 18 (UP), Kirkendall-Spring/Nature Picture Library; 18 (CTR), Water Rights/Alamy Stock Photo; 18 (LO), marinuse - Underwater/Alamy Stock Photo; 19 (UP), Jeff Rotman/Nature Picture Library; 19 (CTR), David Liittschwager/National Geographic Creative; 19 (LO), Sue Daly/Nature Picture Library; 21, Steve Oldham/Getty Images; 22, Visuals Unlimited, Inc./Patrick Smith/Getty Images; 23 (UP), Biophoto Associates/Science Source; 23 (LO), Robert and Jean Pollock/Science Source; 24 (UP), Foodcollection/Getty Images; 24 (LO), Mauro Rodrigues/Shutterstock; 25, Keith Ladzinski/National Geographic Creative; 25 (inset), BrendanHunter/Getty Images; 26-27, Suzanne Goodwin/Alamy Stock Photo; 28-29, Givenworks/Getty Images; 30 (LE), Sue Daly/Nature Picture Library; 30 (RT), Bugsy/Dreamstime; 31 (UP LE), Dennis Laumark/Shutterstock; 31 (UP RT), Ferenc Cegledi/Shutterstock; 31 (LO LE), Alex Mustard/2020VISION/Nature Picture Library; 31 (LO RT), John Seaton Callahan/Getty Images; 32 (UP LE), Christopher Halloran/Shutterstock; 32 (UP RT), Konrad Wothe/Getty Images; 32 (LO LE), Steve Oldham/Getty Images; 32 (LO RT), Andia/UIG via Getty Images; header, Apolinarias/Shutterstock; vocab, Alexander Raths/Shutterstock

**National Geographic supports K–12 educators with ELA Common Core Resources.
Visit natgeoed.org/commoncore for more information.**

Printed in the United States of America
22/WOR/2

Table of Contents

Watery World

Have you ever been to a rocky beach? Sometimes there are small areas of water on the shore. If you peek in, what do you see?

A little ocean world in a tide pool!

Tide Pool Talk

TIDE: The rising and falling of the sea level, usually two times a day

Two Tides

At high tide, the sea is at its highest level. Most of the shore is covered with water.

As waves roll in, they may crash against the shore.

Mont Saint-Michel in France at high tide

At low tide, the sea is at its lowest level. The waves don't reach as high on the shore.

The water is farther out than it was at high tide.

Mont Saint-Michel in France at low tide

At low tide, some water from the high tide gets left behind.

The water stays in low spots.
These are called tide pools.

Who Lives Here?

spider conch

Many animals and seaweeds live in a tide pool. It's a great place to live. Waves bring new food every day. Lots of sun helps seaweeds to grow.

limpet

crab

sea urchin

Sea stars, sea urchins, and seaweeds live in this tide pool.

Tide Pool Talk

SEAWEEDS: Living things found in water that look like plants, but do not have stems, roots, or leaves

Some crazy-looking critters live in tide pools. Many are colorful. Some are spiky. A few have long arms, and others have frills. These animals can be easy to spot.

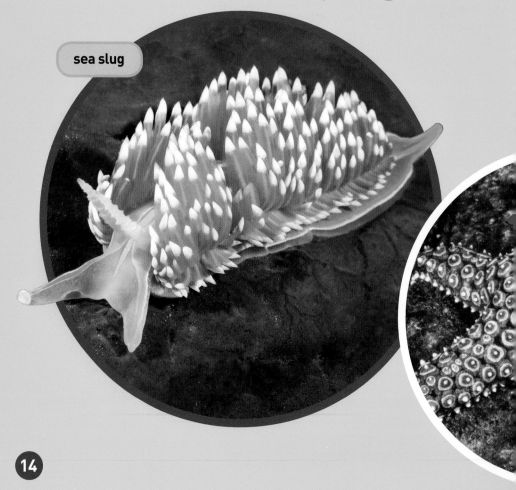

sea slug

chiton (KY-ton)

sea star

sea anemone (uh-NEM-uh-nee)

This sculpin (SKULL-pin) fish blends in with what's around it.

Other animals are hard to spot. This keeps them safe from being eaten.

Some don't even look like animals. But they are! Mussels and barnacles (BARN-ih-kulls) cling to rocks.

barnacles

mussels

6 COOL FACTS About Tide Pool Animals

A giant green sea anemone swallows its prey whole.

1

2

A male sea spider cares for his young. He holds the eggs safely with his legs.

An octopus can travel over land. It may leave a tide pool to search for food.

3

4

A sea cucumber has tube feet around its mouth. It catches food with its feet.

5

An abalone is a large snail. It breathes through the row of holes in its shell.

6

A hermit crab has five pairs of legs. Its two back pairs grip the shell on the inside.

Tide Pool Talk

PREY: An animal that is eaten by another animal

Built to Survive

A tide pool is always changing. Water flows out. The sun warms the tide pool. It may dry out. Then new, cool water rushes in.

Living things must be strong to survive here.

Tide Pool Talk

SURVIVE: To stay alive

One danger is how the water
moves. It rushes in and out. It can
wash away living things. So they
need to stick to the rocks.

Lots of seaweeds have anchors (ANK-ers) that hold them in place. Many animals grip with sticky tube feet. Other living things have threads.

Threads on a mussel keep it in place, so it won't wash away.

The anchors on this seaweed grip the rock.

Drying out is another danger. So plants and animals have ways to stay wet.

Lots of animals close their shells or bodies. This keeps water inside. Others stay wet by hiding under seaweeds.

A sea snail can pull its body inside its shell.

A mussel closes its shell.

Underwater, a green sea anemone opens to stretch out its tentacles.

Out of water, the anemone's tentacles roll up inside its body.

A sea star's body helps it survive. Here's how:

SPINY SKIN protects the sea star from harm.

EYESPOTS at the tip of each arm sense light. They help find food.

TUBE FEET on its underside act like suckers. They help the sea star to eat, move, and stay in one place.

ARMS can open the shells of mussels and clams. Sea stars eat the insides. An arm can grow back if it gets cut off.

A **MOUTH** is used to eat, of course. But this one is not like yours! A sea star's stomach pushes out of its mouth. Its stomach enters the shell of another animal to eat it.

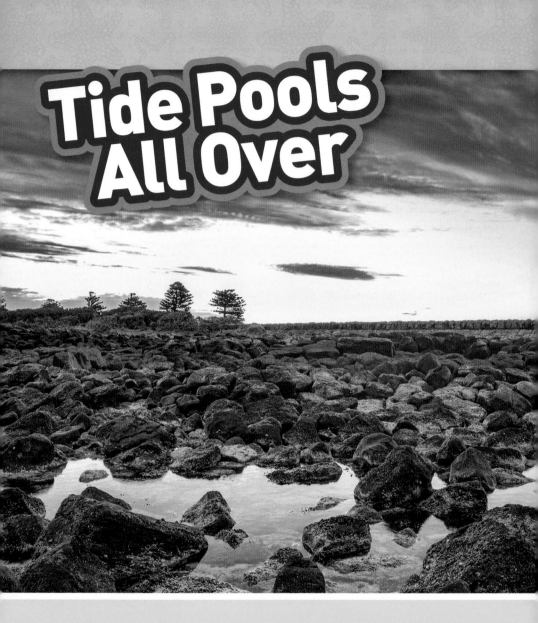

Tide Pools All Over

You'll find tide pools all over the world. They are in cool areas and warm areas.

The plants and animals in them can be different. But many are the same. Tide pools are great places to explore!

What in the World?

These pictures show up-close views of different things. Use the hints to figure out what's in the pictures. Answers are on page 31.

1

2

HINT: These help an animal stick to the rocks.

HINT: These may crash against the shore.

seaweeds   sea star   barnacles   waves   hermit crab   tube feet

3

HINT: Animals hide under these to stay wet.

4

HINT: This animal can grow back an arm if it's cut off.

5

HINT: It has five pairs of legs.

6

HINT: These animals cling to rocks.

Answers: 1. tube feet, 2. waves, 3. seaweeds, 4. sea star, 5. hermit crab, 6. barnacles

PREY: An animal that is eaten by another animal

SEAWEEDS: Living things found in water that look like plants, but do not have stems, roots, or leaves

SURVIVE: To stay alive

TIDE: The rising and falling of the sea level, usually two times a day